MESSI

Abbeville Press Publishers
New York · London

A portion of the book's proceeds are donated to the **Hugo Bustamante AYSO Playership Fund,** a national scholarship program to help ensure that no child misses the chance to play AYSO Soccer. Donations to the fund cover the cost of registration and a uniform for a child in need.

Text by Illugi Jökulsson

For the original edition
Design and layout: Ólafur Gunnar Guðlaugsson

For the English-language edition
Editor: Joan Strasbaugh
Production manager: Louise Kurtz
Designer: Ada Rodriguez
Copy editor: Ken Samuelson

PHOTOGRAPHY CREDITS

Getty Images
11. Messi's Family: AFP. 16. Carles Rexach: Stringer. 26-27. A Celebration: Luis Bagu. 30–31. Eiður and Messi: Jasper Juinen. 36–37. Messi in an international game: Bob Thomas. 38–39. Maradona and Messi: Chaun Botterill. 44–45. The competitors: Victor Carretero. 46–47. Messi and Eiður: Luis Bagu. 52–53. Messi and Antonella: Robert Marquardt. 55. Eiður and Messi: Dennis Doyle. 58–59. Messi and Antonella: Europa Press.

AFP
11. Messi's Family: AFP.+

Shutterstock
Front cover and back cover
2, 3, 6, 8, 9, 10, 11, 12, 13, 14, 15, 16, 17, 18, 19, 20, 21, 22, 23, 24, 25, 27, 28, 29, 32, 33, 34, 35, 40, 41, 42, 43, 48, 49, 50, 51, 52, 53, 54, 55, 56, 57, 61.

All statistics current through the 2012–2013 season unless otherwise noted.

First published in the United States of America in 2014 by Abbeville Press, 137 Varick Street, New York, NY 10013

First published in Iceland in 2012 by Sögur útgáfa, Fákafen 9, 108 Reykjavík, Iceland

First edition
10 9 8 7 6 5 4 3 2 1

Library of Congress Cataloging-in-Publication Data

Illugi Jvkulsson.
  [Lionel Messi. English]
  Messi / by Illugi Jvkulsson.—First edition.
    pages cm. — (World soccer legends)
  Translated from Icelandic.
  Summary: "Profiles the Argentinean soccer star of FC Barcelona, Lionel Messi. Discusses his early childhood success, his training with the Barcelona junior team, and features fun facts like his favorite foods and his pet peeves"— Provided by publisher.
  Includes bibliographical references and index.
  ISBN 978-0-7892-1164-4 (hardback)—ISBN 0-7892-1164-5 (hardcover) 1. Messi, Lionel, 1987—Juvenile literature. 2. Soccer players—Argentina—Biography—Juvenile literature. I. Illugi Jvkulsson. Lionel Messi. Translation of: II. Title.
  GV942.7.M398I45 2014
  796.334092—dc23
  [B]
                    2013045843

For bulk and premium sales and for text adoption procedures, write to Customer Service Manager, Abbeville Press, 137 Varick Street, New York, NY 10013, or call 1-800-ARTBOOK.

Visit Abbeville Press online at **www.abbeville.com.**

CONTENTS

SIMPLY THE BEST!

Frank Rijkaard, Barcelona coach 2003–2008

"It's amazing what Messi can do with the ball. And he's still young and that's great news because that means he can only get better as a soccer player. Soccer should make people happy and that's what Messi does, he makes people happy, he makes people enjoy the game."

Pep Guardiola, Barcelona coach 2008–2012

"Messi is the best. I think I've been very fortunate to have been his coach. He is a unique soccer player. The throne is his. Only he decides when he steps down."

Where Is He From?

Lionel Messi was born on June 24, 1987, in Rosario, the third largest city in Argentina.

VENEZUELA

COLOMBIA

BRAZIL

BOLIVIA

CHILE

PARAGUAY

Rio de Janeiro

Rosario

URUGUAY

Buenos Aires

Montevideo

ARGENTINA

Argentina

The country is in South America and is very big—the eighth largest country in the world. In fact, it covers an area as large as the following 12 European countries combined: Iceland, Norway, Sweden, Denmark, Germany, the Netherlands, Belgium, France, Britain, Ireland, Spain, and Portugal. Yet the population is "just" roughly 40 million. That's slightly smaller than the population of Spain and somewhat larger than the population of Poland. The population of Argentina is the third largest in South America, after Brazil and Colombia. The capital city is called Buenos Aires.

A Turbulent History

The first inhabitants were Indians who settled the south of South America several thousands of years ago. Around 1500 AD the Spaniards started colonizing the continent, and believing that there were great sources of silver to be found in the area they named it *Argentina*— which translates into "Land of Silver." They turned out to be wrong, there was in fact little silver in Argentina, but the name stuck.

Rosario, where Messi was born. 1.2 million people live there.

In 1816 the people broke with Spain and founded a republic. People emigrated from many European countries to Argentina, but Spanish remained the main language.

Argentina has seen some troubled times: the country's history is marred by violent disputes and unrest. The country was, for instance, ruled by the *Junta*, a tyrannical military government from 1976 to 1983. At that time a certain young couple was settling down and starting a family in the city of Rosario.

Messi's parents, Jorge and Celia, with his fiancée Antonella.

The Messi Family

This young couple were Jorge Messi and Celia Cuccittini. He worked in a steel factory and she held various jobs in addition to taking care of the home. In 1980 they had a son called Rodrigo. Another boy was born in 1982 and was given the name Matías. Jorge and Celia were ordinary, diligent working class people with very little money to spare.

Their third son was born in 1987. He was a normal boy who had a very normal childhood. His father and brothers were great soccer enthusiasts, as most Argentinians are, but the little one didn't seem very keen. He preferred to play with glass marbles and collect picture cards.

A Fateful Day

When the boy was four years old his father and brothers were out in the street playing soccer in front of their house. Surprisingly, the little one waddled out and wanted to join in, and of course he was welcome to. His father and brothers were in for a bigger surprise.

"We were shocked to see how good he was," Jorge said later. "And he'd never played before."

This was the first time, but definitely not the last, that the boy charmed people with his ball skills. Because this little boy was Lionel Messi.

The Little Lion, Crab, and Rabbit

Hello!

In 1984 the popular singer Lionel Ritchie released the single "Hello" and it topped the charts worldwide. This was a slow and romantic song that appealed especially to people in love.

Jorge and Celia Messi probably slow-danced a few times to this song when they went out dancing. Three years after the song was released they had their third son and, as the story goes, they decided to name him after the singer.

The name Lionel means "little lion" and fits Lionel Messi perfectly!

Lionel
Ritchie

Sensitive and Caring

Lionel Messi was born on June 24, which means that his zodiac sign is Cancer. People born between June 22 and July 22 all belong to the sign of Cancer.

Some believe that people's zodiac sign determines a lot of people's character and

Riquelme and he was born June 24, 1978. The two of them used to play together on the Argentina national team.

Riquelme is an attacking midfielder with fantastic skills and he was in fact playing for Barcelona when Messi first arrived there. Riquelme was then transferred to Villarreal in Spain, and later to Boca Juniors in Argentina. He has nothing but praise for his young compatriot. "He's simply a genius," Riquelme says of Messi. "The most amazing thing is that he runs faster with the ball than without it. I don't know anyone else that can do that."

Juan Ramán Riquelme.

personality. That's most probably only superstition but people born under this sign are said to be sensitive, very caring, and intuitive. And even though they do enjoy the company of others, they are also very independent.

Messi's Chinese zodiac sign is the rabbit. Rabbits are said to be good friends, generous, friendly, artistic, humble, stubborn, and slightly moody.

Shared Birthday

The most famous soccer player who shares Messi's birthday happens to be an Argentine as well. His name is Juan Ramán

Boy Wonder

When Messi was a boy his grandmother used to take care of him while his parents were at work. She would often take his older brothers to soccer practice and Messi would tag along. He had just started playing with the ball at home and was obviously talented and passionate. However, he was rather short for his age and not very powerfully built.

One day one of the teams was missing one player. It's not clear whether it was the coach or Messi's grandmother who suggested that little Messi should play with the older boys, but he was led to the field. He was shy and timid but wanted to play with the ball.

Messi's grandmother and the coach decided that it would be best to have him play along the sideline so it would be easy to call him off the field if the older boys hurt him and made him cry.

The first time the ball passed to Messi nothing happened. He caught the ball with his right foot and didn't know what to do with it. The ball just bounced away. But the next time he caught the ball with his left foot and the little guy took off. Messi surged down the field with the ball and when one of the big boys came running to take the ball off him, little Messi dodged him easily.

The coach figured he got lucky and yelled at Messi to pass the ball. But the boy just kept on running, taking on one player after another. None of them managed to get the ball off him. His grandmother and the coach watched in awe. They both knew that they'd witnessed the birth of a new genius.

At the age of five Messi started to play with a small club coached by his dad in Rosario called Grandoli. Soccer fever ran deep within the close-knit Messi family. Soon stories of the talented youngster spread and in 1995 he was training with Newell's Old Boys, the largest club in Rosario.

Everyone could see that the boy had great potential. The trouble was that he didn't seem to grow normally and was by far the smallest boy his age. It turned out that he suffered from growth-hormone deficiency and chances were that he would always be very short. And obviously far too small to make it to the very top.

The solution was to give Messi daily hormone injections. He didn't enjoy it but he bit the bullet and from the age of nine Messi could give himself the injections. He started to grow again but the shots were expensive and the Messi family didn't have the means to pay for them. Newell's Old Boys covered the costs.

In 2000 Argentina suffered a bad financial crash, similar to the one that would hit globally in 2008. Money disappeared; everyone had to cut back on spending. Newell's Old Boys could no longer afford to pay for Messi's hormone injections. The boy was thirteen years old and still very small for his age. He would likely never grow to his full height.

Messi was very fond of his grandmother Celia, who used to take him to his first soccer practices. He was devastated when she died in 1998. He honors her memory by raising his finger to the sky after scoring a goal.

Two Great Talents

Incredibly enough, Messi's childhood coaches insist that there was another boy in the same school who matched him in skill and potential. He was called Gustavo but was not as fortunate as Messi, who came from a loving and supportive family. The boys both lived in poor neighborhoods in Rosario and some young people ended up in crime or took to drink and drug abuse. Gustavo's family was not able to give him the support he needed to develop his talents. Bit by bit he lost his way and finally succumbed to alcohol and drugs, his talent wasted and gone. The two boys thus have very different stories. Lionel Messi had a caring family that supported him in every way possible, and he became the greatest soccer player in the world. Gustavo, however, is lost to all.

Barcelona!

F C B

The future didn't look too good for Lionel Messi. It seemed like he would have to quit his hormonal treatment, which in turn meant he would remain quite small and never manage to reach the top league of soccer players. He had little interest in anything else; he was but an average student, although he did show some artistic talent.

But suddenly events took an unexpected turn. Two men who had read reports in the local papers in Rosario on the young—but short—genius, came to see the family. They had been in contact with the great Spanish soccer club FC Barcelona and said they could arrange for Messi to have a trial with the team.

If Messi could get a contract with Barcelona, the club would foot his medical bills so he could reach a normal height. It also meant he would be able to do what he was clearly meant to do—play soccer.

Messi's father flew with his son to Spain where he trained for a week with the club's junior team in September 2000. Anyone could see that the boy was almost ridiculously talented, but did it make sense to bet on a little kid from Argentina not knowing how he would grow and mature?

Without hormone injections

4' 8"

Carles Rexach

The coaches of the junior and cadet teams could not reach a decision. They waited for Carles Rexach to return. He was the manager of the club and was abroad that first week when the Messis were in town. When Rexach returned

Carles Rexach.

With hormone injections

5' 6½"

Messi was playing in a game. Rexach watched in awe as he walked around the field to where the coaches sat. "It took me seven minutes," he later said. "And when I sat down on that bench I had made my decision. I said to the coaches: *We have to sign him. Now.* For what did I see? A kid who was very small, but totally different from anyone else. He had incredible confidence, agility, speed, great technique; he could run full speed with the ball, dodging anyone in his way without hesitation. It wasn't difficult to spot; these talents everyone now know were obvious, even though he was just thirteen years old. Some soccer players need a good team to flourish, but not Messi. People sometimes say that I discovered Messi, but that's nonsense. His talents were there for all to see. If a Martian who'd never seen a game of soccer would have watched Messi play, he would still have understood that this kid was one of a kind."

Everyone seemed happy. Jorge Messi and Lionel went back to Argentina and the family started to prepare the move to Barcelona. It was clear that they would not go unless everyone in the family agreed. The three boys now had a sister named Marisol who had been born in 1995. Everyone was on board; this was a chance of a lifetime for the Little Lion and they had to take it.

A Contract on a Napkin

After a few months, Messi's agents were growing restless waiting for the contract. They went to Rexach and told him to get the papers in order because Real Madrid was showing interest in the young Messi, and they were ready to start negotiations. Rexach didn't hesitate: he grabbed the next piece of paper he got his hands on, a paper napkin. He drew up a contract on the napkin and signed it. And that was how Lionel Messi, at the tender age of thirteen, was signed to FC Barcelona. In February 2001 the whole Messi family arrived in Barcelona and Lionel could start training with his new teammates.

In 1899 a young immigrant from Switzerland had settled in Barcelona. His name was Joan Gamper and had learned to play soccer in his native country. He took out an ad in the paper asking if there were any young men who would like to join him in establishing a soccer team. Eleven people showed up and Futbol Club Barcelona was born.

The club gradually became a force to be reckoned with. The Spanish Championship, La Liga, was founded in 1929. Barça won the championship, Real Madrid ending up in second place.

These two clubs have since been dominant in Spanish soccer. From 1953–1969 Real Madrid reigned supreme, claiming the title 11 times over this 16-year period. Spain's dictator, Francisco Franco, was a fan of the club, and it acquired many of the strongest players in the world.

But Barça was never far behind, and during the season of 1990–1991 the team took off. The coach was the Dutchman Johan Cruyff who assembled the so-called "Dream Team" that won La Liga for four consecutive seasons. Another Dutchman, Louis van Gaal, brought home the title twice just before 2000, but then the club hit a slump and didn't win any titles for five years.

In 2003 the club hired yet another Dutchman, Frank Rijkaard, in the hopes of turning things around. And it worked; Barcelona won two championship titles and beat Arsenal 2–1 in the European Champions League final in 2005–2006. But then Barça seemed to lose focus, and Rijkaard left in 2008.

The next coach was a former Barcelona player who had been coaching Barcelona's junior team. With Pep Guardiola the club rose to great heights. He developed even further the impressive passing game that had become Barcelona's forte, and into the pivotal role of forward moved his best player: Lionel Messi.

The Tr

Catalonia

Barcelona is the capital city of a region in Spain called Catalonia. Catalans have their own language—Catalan—that is closely related to Spanish (Castilian). Catalans are very proud of their identity and like to keep the government in Madrid at an arm's length. Catalonia covers an area that is slightly larger than Belgium. It has a population of 7.5 million and roughly 2 million live in the capital Barcelona.

FRANCE

PORTUGAL

Catalonia

Barcelona

Madrid

Mallorca

The Mediterranean

umphant Barça

Messi celebrating with his teammates, just one of the guys. Can you spot him? In spite of his tremendous individual skill, he always stresses that soccer is a team sport!

The old farmhouse "La Masia" is right beside Camp Nou.

The Flea of La Masia

It was clear that the young Lionel Messi was in the right place as soon as he came to Barcelona. No other club takes as excellent care of its younger teams as Barça does.

Since 1979, the club's soon-to-be celebrated youth academy was based in a 300-year-old country house by Camp Nou called La Masia or "the farm."

For the past 30 years Barça has focused on rearing homegrown virtuosos rather than simply buying skilled players from other clubs.

Pep Guardiola is one of many players who went through the La Masia soccer school. He became FC Barcelona's main midfielder between 1990–2001, and then became a coach with the club, at first with the junior teams and then with the senior team.

La Masia emphasizes pinpoint-accurate passes and collaboration between teammates. Everyone has to work together. This is how Barcelona manages its incredible ball possession during games. The passes tend to be unbelievably accurate and sometimes the team can keep the ball for great lengths of time until someone finds a gap in the opposing team's defense. And then, in a second, the defense is ripped open with magnificent play.

This is what Barcelona players learn in La Masia. It's usually called "tiki-taka." This sort of game suits a skilled player like Messi perfectly. Few players are as good at keeping the ball as he is. Even though he was now growing normally again he was still rather short and was therefore often called La Pulga, or "The Flea."

Alongside Messi, there were other youngsters of the same age in La Masia, such as the defender Gerard Piqué and the midfielder Cesc Fàbregas. The three of them played together for a few seasons until Piqué transferred to Manchester United and Fàbregas to Arsenal. Messi stayed with Barça and kept on sharpening his skills and maturing as a player in La Masia.

Fàbregas and Piqué are now back in Barcelona and the trio now plays together once again.

The Best of Barcelona

Even though Barcelona has always prided itself in rearing its own players, many world-renowned players from abroad have worn the Blaugrana jersey.

Johan Cruyff was one of the greatest soccer players of his time when he joined Barça in 1973. He played for the club for five years and became a successful coach later on with the club.

In 1982 Diego Maradona, who at the time was the most expensive player in the world, joined FC Barcelona. He won the Spanish Cup and scored beautiful goals, but suffered injuries and got into disputes with the club's management and only stayed for two years.

The incredible scorer Romário from Brazil played for Barça from 1993–1995. He scored hundreds of goals in his career, and some exceptional ones in the blue and scarlet uniform of Barcelona.

In 1996 another amazing Brazilian striker joined Barcelona. Ronaldo Nazário scored 47 goals in 51 games, but he left the club after one season. A few years later he joined the ranks of Barça's archrival, Real Madrid.

Luís Figo committed the same "sin." He was a brilliant winger who played for Barça from 1995–2000. He was one of the best players in the world and a fan favorite. But in 2000 he chose to move to Real Madrid, causing bitter outrage among Barça fans.

The Brazilian **Rivaldo** was one of Barça's very best from 1997–2002, scoring some fantastic goals. He was still playing (and scoring goals) with a club in Brazil in 2013, at the age of forty-one.

Taking over from Rivaldo was his countryman **Ronaldinho** who played for Barça between 2003–2008. He was a wizard with the ball, playing with great passion and joy. He knew endless tricks, made perfect passes, fantastic free kicks, and breathtaking goals. The young **Lionel Messi** learned a great deal from this incredible player.

Ronaldinho was an extremely colorful player.

Home Ground!

Barcelona plays its home games in the magnificent Camp Nou stadium. It was inaugurated in 1957 and the name simply means "new ground" in Catalan. The stadium seats 99,354 people. Just to put that into perspective, there are five independent countries in Europe with smaller populations than that! The stadium is always sold out and atmosphere is incredible. No wonder Lionel Messi can't imagine playing anywhere else.

Fifth Largest

Even though Camp Nou is massive it's still "just" the fifth largest stadium in the world. The largest is in North Korea—seating 150 thousand people. Then there are stadiums in India, Mexico, and Iran. Santiago Bernabéu, home to rivals Real Madrid, is considerably smaller than Camp Nou, seating 85,000 people.

Breaking Records

Lionel Messi soon made a name for himself with Barcelona's Juvenil and Cadet teams. The hormone treatments were successful and he was growing and gaining strength. Frank Rijkaard, who took over as coach in 2003, believed in the young Argentine. Messi had proved to be quite the goal scorer and in November 2003 he debuted with Barcelona's first team in a friendly match against Porto. He was 16 years old.

On October 16, 2004, Messi debuted in La Liga with Barça's first team. It was

Barcelona's captain Puyol and his players celebrate the young Messi's first goal against Albacete. Messi is embraced by Mexican defensive stalwart Rafael Márquez.

a game against Espanyol, the city's second largest club. Messi was 17 years old and was the youngest player to play for Barça in La Liga. He played several games with the team during that season and on December 7 he played his first game in the European Champions League. It was in the city of Donetsk in the Ukraine where Barça lost to the home team, Shakthar.

On May 1, 2005, Messi scored his first goal for Barcelona's senior team. The club was playing Albacete in Camp Nou. He came on for Samuel Eto'o, who was Barca's reigning scorer at the time. Messi had a great connection with the Brazilian genius Ronaldinho, who was in Barça's frontline. Shortly after Messi came on he flipped the ball over Albacete's goalkeeper after an assist from Ronaldinho. The referee claimed he was offside and wouldn't count the goal as valid, which was a questionable call.

But Ronaldinho and Messi simply repeated the feat and Messi scored his first valid senior goal in injury time. He was the youngest player to score for the club. Both Barça players and fans went wild because everyone could sense that this was a historic moment in Camp Nou.

Bojan Krkic.

Not All Records Stood for Long

Messi's record of being the youngest to play and score for Barça in La Liga did not last long. During the 2007–2008 season the young Bojan Krkic broke both records. He was born August 28, 1990. Some believed he might even become better than Messi but that was not to be. After a few good years Bojan seemed to hit a slump and he went to Roma in Italy. He is currently playing for the Dutch team Ajax. But there is always a chance he'll return to Barça one day.

Favorites

Milanesa a la Napolitana

Messi loves traditional Argentinian food cooked by his parents.

A strong favorite is *Milanesa a la Napolitana* or Neapolitan-style schnitzel. Messi's mother, Celia, cooks it somehow like this:

She takes slices of beef, thins them with a meat-hammer, sprinkles on salt, dips them into whisked eggs, and covers them in breadcrumbs.

She then fries them in a shallow pan until they are a lovely golden brown and places them into an oven.

While the schnitzel is in the oven, Celia fries sliced onions until they soften and turn yellow, then she adds chopped tomatoes, a bit of water, salt, dried oregano, and a pinch of sugar. She allows this to simmer for 20 minutes, and then the mixture is poured over the meat. Take care to cover it completely.

The whole thing is topped off with slices of cheese, or even cream cheese, before it is returned back into the oven. While the cheese melts, Celia fries some chips, which she serves with the schnitzel.

Messi gobbles this up with delight! And it must be good for you, otherwise such a healthy sports hero would hardly eat it!

Favorite Dessert:

Dulce le leche. Pudding made by slowly simmering milk and sugar, reminiscent of runny caramel.

Favorite Movies:
There are two: *Son of the Bride*— a dramatic comedy about a man and his mother who suffers from Alzheimer's. This movie reminds Messi of his beloved grandmother who suffered a similar illness. The other movie is called *Nine Queens* and is a clever crime story about two con artists. Both movies star Ricardo Darín, one Argentina's most popular movie stars.

Favorite Book:
Diego Maradona's biography. Messi has yet to finish it, and he owns up to being a lazy reader. Sometimes he does, however, mention a long epic poem from Argentina called *El Martín Fierro* that describes an almost "wild west" atmosphere in Argentina in the 19th century.

Favorite Music:
Argentine Cumbia music. Fast and passionate South American dance music. Find it on YouTube!

Superstition:
Messi will not admit to any superstitions but he insists on playing with wet hair.

What He Hates:
Injustice and ill treatment of the poor.

In the Champions League final of 2009 Messi scored Barcelona's second goal against Manchester United with a rare header. Edwin van der Sar looks on in horror!

Messi became a regular with Barcelona's senior team during the 2005–2006 season, even though he was only 18 years old. He later said of Frank Rijkaard, who was coach at the time: "I will never forget that he launched my career and that he had confidence in me even though I was very young."

On November 2, 2005, Messi scored his first goal in the UEFA Champions League against the Greek club Panathinaikos. He scored a total of eight goals that season but suffered an injury in the last months, sadly causing him to miss the final when Barça beat Arsenal 2–1.

Barça's most lethal attackers around this time were Ronaldinho from Brazil, Frenchman Thierry Henry, and especially the famed scorer Samuel Eto'o from Cameroon.

They all left in 2008 and 2010. Messi can be said to have replaced them all! When Messi scored Barcelona's second goal in its 2–0 victory against Manchester United on the May 27, 2009, he sealed the Champions League title for his club.

In the coming years, coach Pep Guardiola built up such a magnificent team around Messi that he couldn't stop scoring fabulous goals! It was clear as day that Messi was taking his place among the greatest and most successful soccer players in history.

Messi is famous for his soccer feints and tricks. He insists he doesn't especially practice these; they become instinctive when you constantly have the ball at your feet at training.

An Epic Goal!

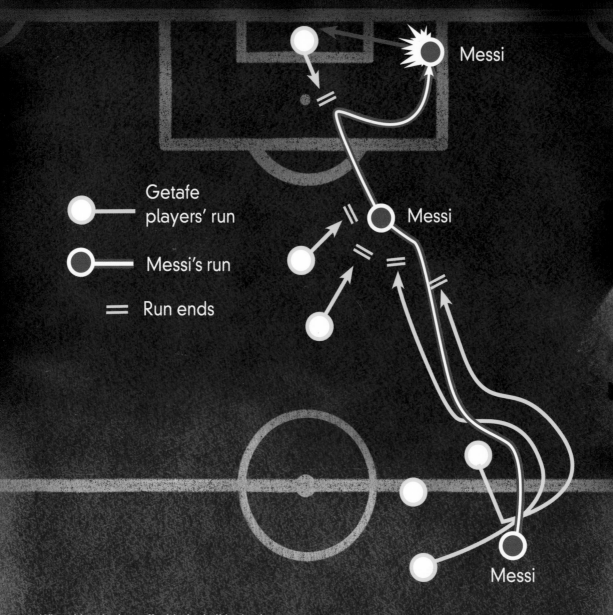

Getafe players' run

Messi's run

= Run ends

Messi

Messi

Messi

When Messi takes off with the ball he is almost unstoppable. No other footballer today can match his ball control. It's worth noting that however many defenders hassle him and try to tackle him, legally or illegally, Messi never takes a dive. He always tries to stay on his feet and keep going. That's where his wizardry comes from.

On April 18, 2007 Messi scored two goals against Getafe in the semifinal of the Spanish Cup, known as Copa del Rey. His second goal is historic. He received the ball from Xavi just behind the halfway line and surged down the field. He shook off five Getafe players, eluded the dive of Getafe's goalkeeper and scored. This epic goal closely resembles a famous goal scored by Diego Maradona against England in the World Cup 1986, dubbed "The Goal of the Century." Messi covered the same length as Maradona (68 yards) and beat six rivals like Maradona. After this stunner Argentina stopped looking for the "next Maradona"—he had obviously arrived. And chances were that he could even surpass the old master! Messi admitted that this goal boosted his confidence. "I may have been overly respectful of my fantastic teammates before and tried to adapt to them. Bit by bit I started taking more control and playing the way I wanted to."

Playing for Argentina

World Cup Champions 1978 and 1986
Won the Copa América 14 times, last time in 1993

The Argentina national soccer team has always been among the strongest national teams in the world. The team appeared in the first final of the World Cup in 1930 when it lost 4–2 to its neighbor, Uruguay. These two teams hold the record for most international matches played between two countries, having faced each other 198 times since 1901.

Argentines also have great soccer rivalry with Brazil. Brazil took the lead when they became World Champions three times between 1958 and 1970, much to the frustration of Argentina. But in 1978 the World Cup was held in Argentina and the national team used the home ground to their full advantage and won the title for the first time. This time they had a powerful team without any superstars. That was to change swiftly when the brightest star of them all arrived on the scene; Diego Maradona excelled during the World Cup in 1986. He scored two goals against England in the quarterfinal that would make soccer history. He scored the first goal by illegally striking the ball into the net with his hand, but the goal stood. After the game Maradona claimed it was the "hand of God" that steered the ball. The second goal is the famous "Goal of the Century" (see pages 32–33) when Maradona received the ball in his own half, dashed towards the English goal, dribbling past five English players and the goalkeeper before smashing the ball into the net.

Many claimed that this goal would never be matched, but in 2007 Messi did just that, matching the Goal of the Century almost touch by touch.

Maradona led his team to Argentina's second World Cup win when they defeated West Germany 3–2 in a tense match. Maradona's contribution was vital and he assisted Jorge Burruchaga for the winning goal in the 84th minute.

MARADONA!

The Argentine Diego Maradona was the greatest soccer player in the world between 1980 and 1990, and was widely regarded as one of the two greatest players of all time.

The other was the Brazilian Pelé who played with three World Cup champions, in 1958, 1962, and 1970.

It's been a long-standing debate who was better: Maradona or Pelé, but now some claim that Messi is better than both of them!

Maradona became addicted to drugs and got into various troubles when he retired from playing, both regarding health issues and the law.

But he managed to pull himself together and became head coach of the Argentina team in 2008, building his team around his successor, Lionel Messi, but was replaced after 2010 World Cup.

Youngest Player in the World Cup

In 2004 Lionel Messi was invited to play for the Spanish national U-20 team, for which he was eligible since he moved to Spain at the tender age of 13. Messi declined the offer because he only wanted to play for Argentina.

In the summer of 2005 Messi led the Argentina U-20 team to victory in the FIFA World Youth Championship. He was the top scorer in the tournament and was awarded both the Golden Ball and the Golden Shoe. Yet he was one of the two youngest players on the squad. Only Sergio Agüero was younger than him. Later that summer Messi made his full international debut in a friendly game against Hungary on August 17, 2005. He had just turned 18 but was already famous for his extraordinary skills, so expectations were high when he came on during the 63rd minute.

But he did not stay long. He got the ball immediately and dribbled easily past a Hungarian defender who was not about to let the young genius leave him in the dust so he tugged at his shirt. Messi batted out an arm to free himself, and his arm landed on the chest or neck of the defender who then took a dive, acting as if Messi had elbowed him in face. Unfortunately the referee fell for it and sent Messi off after roughly 60 seconds on the field.

Fortunately his coach José Pekerman supported Messi and the young man tried to take it on the chin. But back in the locker room Messi broke down in tears, the disappointment was so great.

Two weeks later Messi played his first proper international with the senior team when Argentina took on Paraguay in the 2006 World Cup qualifier. In October he was on the senior team and at the age of 18 he played with Argentine greats such as Hernán Crespo and Juan Ramán Riquelme.

When the Argentina national team was preparing for the 2006 World Cup Messi scored his first international goal. He scored against Croatia in a friendly match on March 1. He then joined the team in Germany for the World Cup. He came on as a substitute in a match against Serbia on June 16, 2006, and scored his first goal in a major international tournament minutes later, the final goal in Argentina's 6–0 victory. He was only 18—the youngest Argentine to represent his country at a World Cup. Even Maradona was older than Messi when he debuted in the World Cup in 1982.

Argentina played very well to begin with but lost to Germany in a penalty shootout in the quarterfinal. Pekerman left Messi on the bench for that match, which he probably shouldn't have.

There were many young promising players debuting in the World Cup 2006. In addition to Messi there were Cristiano Ronaldo from Portugal, Wayne Rooney from England, Robin van Persie from the Netherlands, and Fernando Torres from Spain. None of them was awarded the Best Young Player— that honor went to Lukas Podolski from Germany.

Italy was the dark horse of the tournament and became the unexpected World Champion.

Disappointment at the Copa

The Championship of South America is called the Copa América. Lionel Messi competed for the first time in the Copa in the summer of 2007. Argentina played brilliantly with Riquelme running the show and Crespo, Messi, and Carlos Tévez forming a formidable front line. The team won its first five games and raked in the goals. The magic unexpectedly wore off in the final when the Argentine team broke down and lost 3–0 to an opportunistic Brazil. Messi scored two goals in the Copa 2007 and was voted Best Young Player.

Even the Mighty Fall

Argentina was off to a bad start in the 2010 World Cup qualifying process, and for a while it seemed like the squad would not make it to the finals in South Africa. Much to everyone's surprise, Diego Maradona was asked to take over as coach. He had been the best soccer player in the world and was greatly loved in Argentina. But he had little experience as a coach and there were ups and downs. Maradona had trouble getting Messi and the other brilliant forwards in the squad going. They almost didn't qualify for the tournament. Messi only scored 4 goals in the qualification stage, which counted 18 games.

Once in South Africa however, Argentina and Messi played well, winning all their games at the group stage, and beating Mexico in the Round of 16. Their front line was lethal, with Gonzalo Higuaín and Tévez at the front, Messi right behind them, and Agüero on the substitute bench. Messi didn't score but he was a great playmaker. The World Cup title seemed a very real possibility.

Then disaster struck. In the quarterfinal the Argentine team crumbled when faced with the Germans, and lost 4–0—their biggest loss in the World Cup since 1974. The sting of the blow was especially sore because they had the two geniuses, Messi and Maradona, at the helm. Two of the very best in history!

But there it is. Argentina was out. Maradona was fired. Spain won the title. The Argentines got a chance to patch up their wounded pride a couple of months later when the recently crowned World Champions paid them a visit. Spain and Argentina played a friendly match in Buenos Aires and the Argentines crushed the Spaniards in a 4–1 victory. Messi scored the first of his team's four goals. If only this had been the World Cup final!

Creative

Messi was nominated for the FIFA Golden Ball award in the 2010 World Cup, despite failing to score a goal in the tournament. He was judged to be: "Outstanding in his pace and creativity for his team, dribbling, shooting, passing —spectacular and efficient."

Another Copa Disappointment

Messi's fourth attempt to win a major tournament with the Argentina national team was unsuccessful in the 2011 Copa América. The team did not perform to standard and was eliminated in the quarterfinals after a penalty shootout against Uruguay. Messi did not manage to score a goal in the tournament. He has yet to score a goal in the finals of a major international tournament since 2007.

At the end of August 2013 Lionel Messi had played 82 international games and scored 35 goals. In 2012 he scored 12 goals in 9 games!

Maradona consoles Messi after a devastating World Cup loss to the Germans on the July 3, 2010.

Incredible Years

Even though the going was often tough with the Argentina national team, Messi was always successful with Barcelona. The young player, who because of his size and shyness was not expected to amount to much, was already scoring more goals each season than many other soccer players would be proud to score in an entire career.

2004–2005 La Liga

1	Barcelona	84
2	Real Madrid	80
3	Villarreal	65

Messi 1 goal

UEFA Champions League: Barcelona lost in the Round of 16 to Chelsea. Liverpool claimed the title. Messi did not score in the CL campaign.

Messi scored 1 goal during the season.

2005–2006 La Liga

1	Barcelona	82
2	Real Madrid	70
3	Valencia	69

Messi 6 goals

UEFA Champions League: Barcelona beat Arsenal in the final to claim the title. Messi scored 1 goal.

Messi scored a total of 8 goals during the season.

2006–2007 La Liga

1	Real Madrid	76
2	Barcelona	76
3	Sevilla	71

Messi 14 goals

UEFA Champions League: Barcelona lost in the Round of 16 to Liverpool. AC Milan claimed the title. Messi scored 1 goal.

Messi scored a total of 17 goals during the season.

2007–2008 La Liga

1	Real Madrid	85
2	Villarreal	77
3	Barcelona	67

Messi 10 goals

UEFA Champions League: Barcelona lost in the semifinals to Manchester United who went on to win the title. Messi scored 6 goals.

Messi scored a total of 16 goals during the season.

at Camp Nou

2008–2009 La Liga

1	Barcelona	87
2	Real Madrid	78
3	Sevilla	70

Messi 23 goals

UEFA Champions League: Barcelona beat Manchester United in the final. Messi scored 9 goals.
Top scorer!

Messi scored a total of 38 goals during the season.

2009–2010 La Liga

1	Barcelona	99
2	Real Madrid	96
3	Valencia	71

Messi 34 goals
Top scorer!

UEFA Champions League: Barcelona lost in the semi-finals to Inter Milan who went on to claim the title. Messi scored 8 goals.
Top scorer!

Messi scored a total of 47 goals during the season.

2010–2011 La Liga

1	Barcelona	96
2	Real Madrid	92
3	Valencia	71

Messi 31 goals

UEFA Champions League: Barcelona beat Manchester United in the final. Messi scored 12 goals.
Top scorer!

Messi scored a total of 53 goals during the season.

2011–2012 La Liga

1	Real Madrid	100
2	Barcelona	91
3	Valencia	61

Messi 50 goals
Top scorer!

UEFA Champions League: Barcelona lost in the semi-finals to Chelsea who went on to claim the title. Messi scored 14 goals.
Top scorer!

Messi scored a total of 72 goals during the season.

2012–2013 La Liga

1	Barcelona	100
2	Real Madrid	85
3	Atlético Madrid	76

Messi 46 goals
Top scorer!

UEFA Champions League: Barcelona crashed out in the semi-finals against Bayern Munich which went on to win the title. Messi scored 8 goals.

Messi scored a total of 60 goals during the season.

The Greatest Team of All Time?

Messi is known for his modesty and generosity towards others, both in words and deeds He will always stress that the secret of his success is that he is part of a great team. Some say that the legendary Barça team under the management of Pep Guardiola from 2008 to 2012 was the greatest team of all time. Here are its main players. Those who started out with Barça are tagged like this:

Víctor Valdés

Goalkeeper
Born 1982
Debuted in 2002

For a while many considered Valdés the weakest link in this powerful team. But in fact he won the Ricardo Zamora Trophy, as the best goalkeeper in La Liga, a record 5 times.

Dani Alves

Right defender
Born 1983
Joined Barça in 2008

A great runner and offensive player who scores regularly beautiful long-range goals. He is on the Brazil national team.

Carles Puyol

Central defender
Born 1978
Debuted 1999

Team captain since 2004, a strong leader with great determination and heart. He was also the captain of the Spanish national team.

Gerard Piqué

Center back
Born 1987
Joined 2008

Raised at Barça, then played for 4 years for Manchester United but returned to his roots in 2008. Big and sturdy but surprisingly agile. He's on the Spanish national team. In a relationship with the Colombian singer Shakira.

Eric Abidal

Left defender
Born 1979
With Barça 2007–2013

Rock-solid and strong defender who was greatly appreciated by his teammates. He battled cancer successfully. He represented France in more than 60 international matches.

Sergio Busquets

Midfielder
Born 1988
Debuted 2008

He appeared slightly gawky to begin with but developed into a great defensive midfielder. He is on the Spanish national team.

Xavi

Midfielder
Born 1980
Debuted 1998

One of the top midfielders in the world. His accurate passes and playmaking are phenomenal. He is the key to Barça's superior ball possession and has represented Spain in over 100 international games.

Javier Mascherano

Midfielder
Born 1984
Joined 2010

This captain of the Argentina national team came from Liverpool in 2010. He is fierce on the field and Guardiola tended to use him as a central defender.

Andrés Iniesta

Midfielder
Born 1984
Debuted in 2002

Like Xavi, Iniesta has great ball control and pinpoint-accurate passes. He keeps a low profile but is one of the best soccer players in the world. Iniesta scored the winning goal for Spain when they claimed the World Cup title in 2010.

Lionel Messi

Forward
Born 1987
Debuted 2004

David Villa

Forward
Born 1981
Joined 2010
Left 2013

Top scorer of all time with the Spanish national team. He was injured for the latter part the 2011–2012 season and no doubt the goals he would have scored would have enabled Barça to win La Liga and the Championship that season.

Other stalwarts:

Cesc Fàbregas

Midfielder
Born 1987
Joined 2011

Played with Messi and Piqué in Barça's younger teams before joining Arsenal where he became a star at a young age. He returned to Barça in 2011 and was meant come in for Xavi. He's an impressive attacking midfielder.

Seydou Keita

Midfielder
Born 1980
Played for Barça
2008–2012

Keita is a Mali national. A versatile player with good ball control and a knack for scoring important goals. Guardiola praised him for always being ready and playing with great heart, even though he wasn't always one of the starting eleven.

Pedro

Forward
Born 1987
Debuted 2008

A light and agile forward who scored a total of 45 goals for Barcelona in consecutive seasons starting in 2009–2010. He has been less prominent of late, but that is probably just a temporary spell.

Alexis Sánchez

Forward
Born 1988
Joined 2011

A skilled goal scorer who has been on the Chile national team from the age of 18. He came from Udinese in Italy and had a very good start with the team.

Many new players have come up from La Masia to play with Barça's senior team. Three of the most talented were Thiago Alcantara, Isaac Cuenca, and Cristian Tello, all born in 1991. In the summer of 2013 Thiago left for Bayern Munich.

Pep Guardiola is a great thinker. He left as head coach of Barcelona in 2012, claiming to need a rest after years of intense pressure. His assistant, Tito Vilanova, took over but had to resign a year later, following a serious illness.

Lionel Messi and Cristiano Ronaldo are the current two giants of soccer. They have faced each other numerous times, and Messi has been on the winning side more often than Ronaldo. The rivals have great respect for each other, and it's clear that neither wants to let the other too near on the field. After the 2012–2013 season Messi and Ronaldo had faced off 23 times.

3 matches Barcelona vs. Man. United in 2008 and 2009

Barcelona won 1, United won 1, and there was 1 draw. Messi scored 1 goal.

8 matches Barcelona vs. Real in La Liga 2009–2013

Barcelona won 4, Real won 2, 2 draws. Messi scored 5, Ronaldo 3.

5 matches Barcelona vs. Real in the Copa del Rey

Barcelona won 1, Real won 2, 2 draws. Ronaldo scored 5.

4 matches Barcelona vs. Real in the Spanish Super Cup

Barcelona won 2, Real won 1, 1 draw. Messi scored 5, Ronaldo 2.

2 games Barcelona vs. Real in UEFA Champions League

Barcelona won 1, 1 draw. Messi scored 2 goals.

The Ferocious Rivals

The 17th match was an international one between Argentina and Portugal on February 9, 2011, in Buenos Aires. Ángel di María, Ronaldo's teammate at Real, scored the first goal for Argentina after a spectacular assist from Messi, but Ronaldo evened the score. Messi scored the winning goal from a penalty kick in the 89th minute.

23 Matches

Messi wins	Messi goals	Draws	Ronaldo wins	Ronaldo goals
10	14	7	7	11

Messi's Strengths

Matches between Barcelona and Real Madrid are called "El Clásico." For one of these pivotal matches the BBC asked striker Eidur Gudjohnsen to compare the two star players on the rival teams, Cristiano Ronaldo and LIONEL MESSI.

Gudjohnsen knows both players well, having faced Ronaldo several times when he was with Chelsea, and having been Messi's teammate in Barça for three years—just when Messi was emerging on the scene. See what Gudjohnsen had to say about Messi and how he rated him on various levels.

Technique
The BBC journalist said that Messi's feet are "as sensitive as a pickpocket's hands." He went on to say that no other player has shown that level of ball control. "His bewildering repertoire of feints and swerves, sudden stops and demoralizing spurts leave defenders dumbfounded time and again."

Gudjohnsen: "His control is the best I have ever seen, it is truly breathtaking."

10/10

Heading Ability
Despite his height Messi has scored some memorable headers. Who can forget the second goal in the Champions League final 2009 in Rome when he sealed the victory for Barça against ManU?

Gudjohnsen: "His size is not a problem. You can't afford to underestimate him in the air; if you do, he will find the net."

6/10

Free Kicks
Messi is a good shooter and is capable of exquisite free-kick goals, though he maybe has yet to match his rival's great variations of free kicks.

Gudjohnsen: "He has so much ability and such magic in his feet that he can do anything with a dead ball."

7/10

Team Player

Messi is the ultimate team player and a great part of his success comes down to the beautiful team play between him and the likes of Xavi and Iniesta. He seems to almost read his teammates' minds and selflessly drags defenders away with runs to free up his mates.

Gudjohnsen: "He is the perfect teammate. Quiet, dignified, brilliant to play with."

9/10

Goals

Messi and Ronaldo are the greatest goal scorers of today and possibly of all time. They are both incredible soccer players but the diminutive Argentine unquestionably has that something extra special that we have never seen before.

Gudjohnsen: "It's so hard to say one is better than the other. They are reaching standards that very few of us have seen anyone reach in recent years. But Messi narrowly has the edge. I have never seen anything like him. We'd be lucky to be watching one of them. To be entertained by both is a blessing."

10/10

Messi and Gudjohnsen celebrating Messi's goal against Almeria at Camp Nou in October 2007.

The Golden Boy!

Lionel Messi has been awarded FIFA's highest honor four consecutive times. The award is now called the FIFA Ballon d'Or.

Messi won an earlier version of the award in 2009, becoming the first player to win this prestigious award four times. Dutchmen Johann Cruyff and Marco van Basten, and the Frenchman Michel Platini received the award three times before it was merged with the FIFA World Player of the Year Award in 2010.

We will probably have to wait a long time for someone to win it five times. Unless Messi does it himself!

2006	The award went to the Italian Fabio Cannavaro of Real Madrid. Messi appeared for the first time on the list, in 20th place.	

2007	**Kaká, AC Milan**	**1**
	Ronaldo, ManU	2
	Messi, Barcelona	3

2008	**Ronaldo, ManU**	**1**
	Messi, Barcelona	2
	Torres, Liverpool	3

2009	**Messi, Barcelona**	**1**
	Ronaldo, ManU/Real	2
	Xavi, Barcelona	3
	Iniesta, Barcelona	4
	Eto'o, Barcelona	5

2010	**Messi, Barcelona**	**1**
	Iniesta, Barcelona	2
	Xavi, Barcelona	3
	Sneijder, Inter Milan	4
	Forlán, Atlético Madrid	5

2012	**Messi, Barcelona**	**1**
	Ronaldo, Real Madrid	2
	Iniesta, Barcelona	3
	Xavi, Barcelona	4
	Falcao, Atlético Madrid	5

2011		
Messi, Barcelona		**1**
Ronaldo, Real Madrid		2
Xavi, Barcelona		3
Iniesta, Barcelona		4

An Incredible Record!

Barcelona reclaimed the Spanish championship in 2012–2013 when the team topped La Liga with the fabulous total of 100 points! Barça reigned supreme under the guidance of new coach, Tito Vilanova, especially in the first half of the season. And in 2012 Messi set a new and incredible record by scoring a total of 91 goals for Argentina and Barça. He scored 12 goals in 9 international matches for Argentina, and 79 goals in 60 matches for Barça. The former record was 85 goals in one year and was held by the German Gerd Müller since 1972.

Messi accomplished another remarkable feat on March 2, 2012, when he broke Cesar Rodriguez's record for most goals scored for Barcelona. Cesar's record, which stood for 57 years, was 232 goals but by the end of the 2012–2013 season, Messi had scored 313 goals!

Spanish Super Cup

Two matches against Real Madrid
Aggregate win 5–4
Messi scored **3 goals** and provided two assists.

UEFA Super Cup

One match against Porto.
Final score 2–0.
Messi scored **1 goal** and provided 1 assist.

FIFA Club World Cup

Two games, first against Al Sadd from Qatar and then Santos from Brazil.
Total final score 8–0.
Messi scored **2 goals** and provided 1 assist. He was joint top scorer with teammate Adriano and was voted Best Player.

Copa del Rey

Seven games against Osasuna, Real Madrid, Valencia, and Athletic Bilbao.
Messi scored **3 goals** and provided 4 assists.

Champions League

11 games against AC Milan, BATE Borisov, Viktoria Plzen, Bayer Leverkusen, and Chelsea.

Messi's old friend from La Masia, Cesc Fàbregas, was back with Barca for the 2011–2012 season. Here they are celebrating a goal. Just behind them are Seydou Keita and another old friend, Gerard Piqué.

In the 2012-13 season Messi continued scoring a stunning amount of goals, altogether 60 in 50 games! And the 2013-14 La Liga season began spectacularly, with 5 goals in the first 2 games under new coach and compatriot Gerardo Martino.

Messi scored **14 goals** and provided 5 assists. Scored a total of five goals in one game against Bayer Leverkusen, a record for the Champions League.

La Liga
37 games. Messi scored **50 goals** and provided 15 assists.

With FC Barcelona
60 games
73 goals!
28 assists

5 goals in internationals
In addition to all the goals for Barcelona, Messi played 3 games with his national team during the season and scored **5 goals**, counting a hat trick in a friendly match against Switzerland. Messi scored 10 hat tricks during the season, twice four goals in a game, and once five goals in one game.

Great Wealth, Great Generosity

Lionel Messi is not one to flaunt his wealth even though he is of course quite rich. According to statistics Messi is one of the richest and highest paid soccer players in the world. Yet Messi is only around 10th place when it comes to the list of the richest athletes, ranking above him are a few golfers, NBA basketball players and 2–3 tennis players, such as Roger Federer.

Charity

Messi uses his wealth to help vulnerable children. He established the Leo Messi Foundation in 2007 to help poor and sick children worldwide, especially in South America, to realize their dreams. Financial help and support from Messi has enabled numerous children to gain access to education and health care.

Messi has also acted as a goodwill ambassador for UNICEF, a UN program providing help to children in developing countries.

A wall mural depicting Messi in Argentina.

A New Messi?

On November 2, 2012 Messi and his girlfriend Antonella Roccuzzo announced the birth of their son, Thiago. They had been dating for a few years and this was their first child. Messi met Antonella back in Rosario, where he visits as often as possible. "I am the happiest man in the world today," Messi said the day Thiago was born.

Top 10 Highest Paid Soccer Players of 2013

1	David Beckham, LA Galaxy	$50.6 Million
2	Cristiano Ronaldo, Real Madrid	$43.5 Million
3	Lionel Messi, Barcelona	$40.3 Million
4	Sergio Aguero, Man. City	$20.8 Million
5	Wayne Rooney, Man. United	$20.3 Million
6	Yaya Toure, Man. City	$20.2 Million
7	Fernando Torres, Chelsea	$20.2 Million
8	Neymar, Santos	$19.5 Million
9	Ricardo Kaká, Real Madrid	$19.3 Million
10	Didier Drogba, Galatasaray	$17.8 Million

10 Facts

A familiar sight. Defenders rushing towards Messi.

When Messi scored 73 goals in the 2011–2012 season he set a world record of most scored goals in one season. The previous record holder was the Scotsman Archie Stark who scored 70 goals for a U.S. club in the 1920s.

When Ronaldinho left Barça in 2008 Messi inherited his number 10 shirt. Ever since the Brazilian genius Pelé was assigned the number it has been worn by creative playmakers, attacking midfielders or even "second strikers." Maradona always wore the number 10, and now Messi also wears the shirt with the Argentina national team.

Messi signed a contract with the Chinese automobile company Chery to promote the luxury vehicle Riich G5. His favorite sports car, however, is the Ferrari Spyder.

His full name is Lionel Andrés Messi.

During his first seasons with Barcelona Messi was prone to injuries and had to rest for weeks on end. The club's doctors believed that growth spurts due to the hormone treatments were to blame. They developed a series of stretches for him to do and since then Messi has suffered very few injuries.

Messi's parents, Jorge and Celia, once considered moving to Australia where they had

An even more familiar sight. Messi in mid strike.

a better chance of employment than back home in Argentina. Messi was not born at that time. But what would have become of Leo Messi in Australia?

Messi played with the Argentina national team at the 2008 Beijing Olympics. The team won all its matches and beat Nigeria 1–0 in the final. Ángel di María scored the winning goal after an assist from Messi, who scored 2 goals in the games.

Zlatan Ibrahimovic was Messi's teammate at Barça for one season. He did not live up to expectations in Barcelona but he has great respect for Messi. When asked who was better, Messi or Ronaldo, Zlatan answered: "Messi is a natural. Ronaldo is the result of training."

When Messi arrived in Barcelona at the tender age of 13 to try out for the Barça management, his father promised him a new track suit if he scored six goals in the first trial game. Messi scored five but got the track suit anyway as his sixth goal was cancelled for offside.

The first time Messi met Diego Maradona he wanted to ask his idol for an autograph or to have their picture taken together. When he faced Maradona he became so shy that he couldn't utter a word and didn't dare ask for anything.

Looking back.

In 2013 the Argentine Jorge Bergoglio was elected Pope Francis. Messi went to visit his countryman in the Vatican. This photograph was humorously captioned by Messi fans: The Pope meeting God.

Maradona

ow Tall Is He?

Height under bar: 8 feet

6'3"
Andy Carroll

6'1"
Cristiano Ronaldo

6'0"
Gareth Bale

5'1"
Ryan Giggs

Messi is living proof that size doesn't matter. And not just Messi. Some of Barcelona's other greats are also on the shorter side. Xavi and Iniesta are both 5'7" tall and Pedro is the same height as Messi.

5'8"
Sergio
Agüero

5'7"
Lionel
Messi

5'5"
Diego
Maradona

The Future

"Titles and awards please my family and also the people of Barcelona and Argentina, and maybe more. That really means a lot to me. But I'm always just the same guy who simply loves playing around with a ball and who is really lucky to be part of a great team."

Lionel Messi has a humble and quiet demeanor despite always rushing onward and upward. He celebrated his 25th birthday on June 15, 2013, so he is in the prime years of a player's life.

Messi has already had such incredible success with Barcelona that it is hard to imagine how he can progess further. But he claims that he is far from becoming tired of the beautiful game. He also insists that he has no desire to play for another club and would prefer to spend his entire career with Barcelona.

There is no doubt that he still has more to offer the Argentina national team, and his biggest dream is to lift the World Cup. He wants to bring home the trophy to please his fellow countrymen of Argentina.

When he retires he intends to move back home to Rosario and live surrounded by his loved ones.

In the summer of 2013 the hugely promising Brazilian forward Neymar joined Barcelona. He claimed his main objective was to help Messi become an even better player. For soccer fans their co-operation on the field is a mouth-watering prospect.

Learn More!

Books

- *Messi: The Inside Story of the Boy who Became a Legend,* by Luca Caioli
  An insightful, well-written, and entertaining biography.
- *The Flea: The Amazing Story of Leo Messi,* by Michael Part
  Everything you'd want to know about the soccer genius.

Websites

- The **Wikipedia** entry on Messi holds an abundance of information about the player, his life, teammates, and soccer results.
- espnfc.com (Soccernet)
- goal.com
- 101greatgoals.com
- fcbarcelona.com
- messi.com (A fan page)

Glossary

Striker: A forward player positioned closest to the opposing goal who has the primary role of receiving the ball from teammates and delivering it to the goal.

Winger: The player who keeps to the margins of the field and receives the ball from midfielders or defenders and then sends it forward to the awaiting strikers.

Offensive midfielder: This player is positioned behind the team's forwards and seeks to take the ball through the opposing defense. They either pass to the strikers or attempt a goal themselves. This position is sometimes called "number 10" in reference to the Brazilian genius Pelé, who more or less created this role and wore shirt number 10.

Defensive midfielder: Usually plays in front of his team's defense. The player's central role is to break the offense of the opposing team and deliver the ball to their team's forwards. The contribution of these players is not always obvious but they nevertheless play an important part in the game.

Central midfielder: The role of the central midfielder is divided between offense and defense. The player mainly seeks to secure the center of the field for their team. Box-to-box midfielders are versatile players who possess such strength and foresight that they constantly spring between the penalty areas.

Fullbacks (either left back or right back): Players who defend the sides of the field, near their own goal, but also dash up the field overlapping with wingers in order to lob the ball into the opponent's goal. The fullbacks are sometimes titled wing backs if they are expected to play a bigger role in the offense.

Center backs: These players are the primary defenders of their teams, and are two or three in number depending on formation. The purpose of the center backs is first and foremost to prevent the opponents from scoring and then send the ball towards the center.

Sweeper: The original purpose of the sweeper was to stay behind the defending teammates and "sweep up" the ball if they happened to lose it, but also to take the ball forward. The position of the sweeper has now been replaced by defensive midfielders.

Goalkeeper: Prevents the opponent's goals and is the only player who is allowed to use their hands!

Coach:

_____

Pick Your Team!

Who do you want on the field with Messi?
Pick your team and don't forget the coach!

Goalkeeper:

_____

Right back:

_____

Left back:

_____

Defender:

_____

Defender:

_____

Midfielder:

_____

Midfielder:

_____

Midfielder:

_____

Forward:

MESSI

_____

Forward:

_____

Forward:

The Messi Board Game!

Play with one die

Play to win!

And we're off!

2

The coach thinks you're too small and doesn't let you play. Wait 1 round.

You score the first goal with the school team. Go forward 4 places.

5

You're too shy to go to Barcelona. Go back 4 places.

You become the main star in La Masia. Go forward 3 places.

8

You're in the starting 11 but get injured. Wait 1 round.

Argentina loses in the World Cup. You are devastated. Wait 2 rounds.

14

You become champion with Barcelona. Go forward 4 places!

You provide a beautiful assist to Gudjohnsen who scores. Roll again.

11

You score a hat trick for the first time. Go forward 3 places.